MW01103202

GL 1.7
IL K.2
LX NF

How Things Grow

From Caterpillar to Moth

By Jan Kottke

Children's Press
A Division of Grolier Publishing
New York / London / Hong Kong / Sydney
Danbury, Connecticut

Photo Credits: Cover and all photos © Dwight Kuhn

Contributing Editors: Mark Beyer and Eliza Berkowitz
Book Design: MaryJane Wojciechowski

Visit Children's Press on the Internet at:
http://publishing.grolier.com

Library of Congress Cataloging-in-Publication Data

Kottke, Jan.
  From caterpillar to moth / by Jan Kottke.
    p. cm. — (How things grow)
  Includes bibliographical references and index.
  Summary: Simple text and photographs show the evolution of a moth, from its
beginning stages as a caterpillar to an adult.
  ISBN 0-516-23307-6 (lib. bdg.) — ISBN 0-516-23507-9 (pbk.)
  1. Moths—Metamorphosis—Juvenile literature. 2. Caterpillars—Juvenile literature. [1.
Moths. 2. Caterpillars. 3. Insects—Metamorphosis.] I. Title.

QL544.2.K68 2000
595.78'139—dc21

                                                          00-024379

Contents

These are **moth** eggs.

They sit side by side on a leaf.

Caterpillars will **hatch** from these eggs.

5

A baby caterpillar has hatched.

It is very small.

It lives on leaves.

7

The caterpillar is changing.

It is growing larger.

It is now the same color as the leaves.

9

The caterpillar starts to make its **cocoon**.

A cocoon is made from a caterpillar's **saliva**.

The cocoon hangs from a tree branch.

11

The cocoon is finished.

The caterpillar will live inside the cocoon for the winter.

The caterpillar is now a **pupa**.

13

Winter is over.

The pupa has turned into a moth.

The moth comes out of its cocoon.

15

The moth flaps its wings to dry them.

It gets ready to leave the tree and fly away.

17

This is a grown-up moth.

It is sitting on a leaf.

It is looking for a place to lay its eggs.

19

It lays its eggs on a bright green leaf.

It lays three eggs side by side.

Caterpillars will hatch from these eggs.

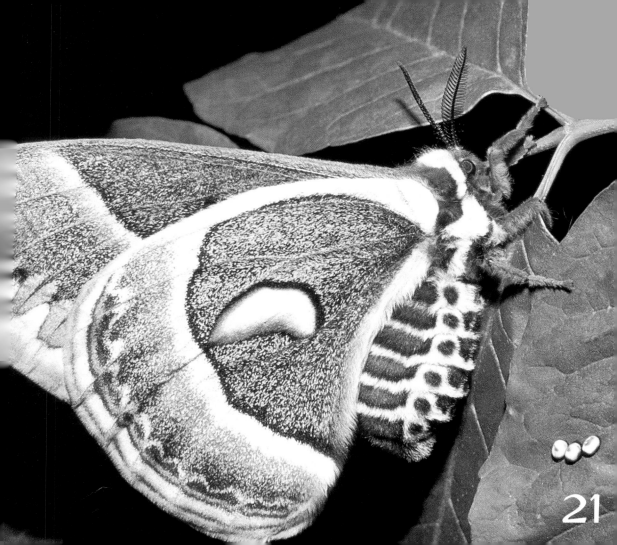

21

New Words

caterpillars (**cah**-ter-**pih**-lerz) insects that turn into moths or butterflies

cocoon (kuh-**koon**) something that caterpillars live in while they are turning into adults

hatch (**hach**) to come out of an egg

moth (**mawth**) a flying insect that starts as a caterpillar

saliva (suh-**lie**-vuh) water made inside the mouth

pupa (**pyoo**-puh) the form of an insect before it becomes an adult

To Find Out More

Books

Butterflies and Moths
by Larry Dane Brimmer
Children's Press

Moth
by Barrie Watts
Silver Burdett Press

I'm a Caterpillar
by Jean Marzollo
Scholastic

Web Sites
Children's Butterfly Site
http://www.mesc.usgs.gov/butterfly/Butterfly.html
This Web site tells the story of a moth's life cycle. It also contains a coloring page and a list of links to other sites.

Most Wanted Bugs
http://www.pbrc.hawaii.edu/~kunkel/wanted
This Web site has information on many different insects, including moths. It also includes fun facts and pictures.

Index

About the Author

Jan Kottke is the owner/director of several preschools in the Tidewater area of Virginia. A lifelong early education professional, she is completing a phonics reading series for preschoolers.

Reading Consultants

Kris Flynn, Coordinator, Small School District Literacy, The San Diego County Office of Education

Shelly Forys, Certified Reading Recovery Specialist, W.J. Zahnow Elementary School, Waterloo, IL

Peggy McNamara, Professor, Bank Street College of Education, Reading and Literacy Program